I'M A LITTLE YOGI

Shirley Barbosa

PALMETTO
PUBLISHING

Charleston, SC
palmettopublishing.com

I'm A Little Yogi
Copyright © 2020 by Shirley Barbosa

ISBN: 978-1-64990-564-2

I'm a little yogi, brave and kind.
Moving and breathing,
I quiet my mind.

My arms extend right from my heart,
hands in prayer, my practice starts.
Three angels breaths to lead the way,
Namaste to start the day.

Breathe in, breathe out, just breathe
and be. Always remember, peace
begins with me. Breathe in, breathe out,
I'll close my eyes. Allow each moment
to be a surprise.

I'm a little yogi, brave and kind.
I'll stand in mountain, lift my arms
to the sky.

Breathing deeply
through my nose,
I'll forward fold
and touch my toes.

Half way lift to monkey pose,
step or jump to my strong plank pose.
Strong arms, strong legs,
pull my belly in then long exhale
to knees, chest, chin.

Up Dog is next,
here I stand on my arms.
I open my heart, and look
up to the sky.
I'm a little yogi,
I feel thankful inside.

I'm a little yogi, brave and kind.
I can move and breathe to quiet my mind.
Now it's time for my favorite pose.
Nice big inhale through my nose.
I lift my hips up to the sky, downward
dog to lengthen my spine.

My head hangs down,
I really feel the pose.
I can wag my tail and
add quick exhales through my nose!
Panting breaths fill me with energy.
I feel alive and so carefree.

Froggy jumps are so fun here,
get really silly for the end
of my practice is near.
Jump one time, two times,
maybe three then find my Mountain.
Breathe and be.

Do nothing pose for final rest.
One hand on my belly, one hand on my
chest. I close my eyes, relax my jaw and
feel my breath just rise and fall.

I'm a little yogi,
peace begins with me.
I thank my body,
it worked so hard for me.
I'll finish up with a giant hug
and squeeze myself
with so much love.

Cross my legs, sit nice and tall,
hands in prayer to finish it all.
I'm a little yogi, brave and kind.
I can move and breathe
to quiet my mind.

NAMASTE

CPSIA information can be obtained
at www.ICGtesting.com
Printed in the USA
LVHW071803291220
674977LV00013B/346